From Everywhere a Little

A Migration Anthology

edited by Dawn Hogue and Lisa Vihos

Water's Edge Press
Sheboygan, Wisconsin

Copyright © 2019 by Water's Edge Press

All rights reserved. This book or any portion thereof
may not be reproduced or used in any manner whatsoever
without the express written permission of the publisher
except for the use of brief quotations in a book review. Poets included in
this anthology retain individual rights to their work.

Printed in the United States of America

ISBN-13: 978-0-9992194-3-0

Library of Congress Control Number: 2019900813

Water's Edge Press
Sheboygan, WI

waters-edge-press.com

Cover image from Getty Images

"I'm not from here
But you're not either
From nowhere entirely
From everywhere a little"
—Jorge Drexler

Contents

Acknowledgments 7
Foreword 9
Introduction 10
    About 100 Thousand Poets for Change 11
From the Reading 13
    Tad Phippen Wente, New Arrivals: 1980 15
    Marilyn Zelke Windau, United in Dream 16
    James Burton, A Part of the Dawn 18
    Maryann Hurtt, Hummus and Hot Dogs 19
    Bobbie Lee Lovell, Lullaby for Troubled Times 20
    Isabel Martinez, Immigrant Poem 21
    Kaitlyn Becker, Fools 22
    Sylvia Cavanaugh, Why Do We Have to Have a Seating Chart? 23
    Georgia Ressmeyer, The Voyage 24
    Ed Werstein, Citizen of the World 27
    Emalie Kamin, You 28
    Scott Allen Schmidt, Cross Copulation 30
    Steven Golden, Beware of Bees During High Wind 32
Leaving and Arriving 35
    Bruce Dethlefsen, Papa's Lullaby 37
    Enesa Mahmić, Sunday Lunch in Exile 38
    Martha Kaplan, Gao Xingjian leaves Beijing 39
    Eneida Alcalde, When You Left 40
    Peggy Trojan, The Immigrant 41
    Nancy Austin, Opportunity 42
    Mary C. Rowin, Intransitives Need No Object 43
    Kathryn Gahl, I Went With My Brother 44
    Jeri McCormick, Journey 45
    Annette Langlois Grunseth, In My Mother's Recipe Box 46
    Jesse Simnegar, Home 47
    Rosalind Brenner, The Hole 48
    Juleigh Howard-Hobson, Mit Patience 50
    Shelley Puhak, Letter to My Great-Grandmother, RE: Her Luck 51

Advice and Prayers 53
    John Guzlowski, Refugees 55
    John Sibley Williams, The Promise 56
    Patrick Cabello Hansel, Driving Without a License 57
    Phyllis Wax, Refugees 58
    Aileen Bassis, Advice for Travelers 59
    Pantea Amin Tofangchi, Phoenix 60
    Mark Zimmermann, Postcard from Ikuno 61
    Aline Mello, If Only Caetano Veloso Knew He Was Singing to Me 62
    Beth Gulley, Prayer Beads 63
    Rob Williams, Skein 64
    Tracey Ludvik, Truth of the Mayan 65
    John Sierpinski, Dobrze (well) 66
    Johanna DeMay, Tribal Identity 67
    Vinita Agrawal, Home is Elsewhere 68
    Jennifer Lagier, First Day of School 69

Seeds and Wings 71
    Mary Jo Balistreri, Sandhill Cranes along the Platte River 73
    Carrie La Seur, The Iowa 74
    Toti O'Brien, Gypsy Steps 75
    Marisa Frasca, Ode to Wild Fennel 76
    Olga Livshin, Translating a Life 78
    Jeremy Griffin, Migration 79
    Sheryl Slocum, Ornamental 80
    Michael Kriesel, Like a Raspberry Seed between my Teeth 81
    Amy Murre, Palm 82
    Joe Amaral, Wildlife Corridors 83
    Jenny McBride, Treeline 84
    Ethel Mortenson Davis, Migrations 85
    Paula Schulz, Monarch Butterflies 86
    Rick Kempa, White Birds 87

About the Contributors 89
About the Editors 95
Coda 97

Acknowledgments

The poems listed below previously appeared in the following publications:

New Arrivals: 1980. "Celebrating Wisconsin People: Wisconsin Poets' Calendar," 2019.
Hummus and Hot Dogs. "Tuck Magazine," 2018.
Citizen of the World. "Peninsula Poets." Poetry Society of Michigan, 2015.
The Immigrant. "Talking Stick." Volume 21, 2012.
Intransitives Need No Object. "you are here: the journal of creative geography." Issue XIX: Memory, 2017.
Journey. "When It Came Time." Salmon Poetry, Ireland, 1998.
Letter to my Great-Grandmother, RE: Her Luck. "South Carolina Review." Spring, 2013.
Refugees (Phyllis Wax). "Echoes of Tattered Tongues: Memory Unfolded." Aquila Polonica, 2016.
Phoenix. "Pomegranate Skin," 2009.
Home is Elsewhere. "The Proverse" anthology, 2017.
Like a Raspberry Seed between my Teeth. "Verse Wisconsin #101," 2010 and "Solitary Plover," Winter, 2014.
Migrations. "I Sleep Between the Moons of New Mexico." New York: iUniverse, Inc., 2010.
Translating a Life. "Rise Up Review." Issue 15, 2019.

Foreword

by Marcos Guevara

the idea works (relentlessthinkers.com) Sheboygan, Wisconsin

In many pre-colonial cultures of Mesoamerica, the butterfly—due to its transformation from caterpillar to chrysalis to its final form—is seen as a symbol of the creation of life and of rebirth. For some, the motion of its wings evokes the movement of a flame: thus, the butterfly is also associated with deities of the sun and summer.

Today, immigration activists often use the monarch butterfly as a symbol because of the multi-generational migration that the butterfly undertakes annually, not only facing the dangerous transit from the South and back, but also defying borders and barriers in order to ensure the prosperity of future generations. And it is not just the monarch that moves in search of shelter and food. Cranes, ducks, even the tiny hummingbird fly well beyond what might be considered "home" in order to fulfill their life's demands.

People are no different. One of the threads in this anthology is the physical migration of people—of how we come from many places, near and far, searching for prosperity, happiness, safety—of how so few of us are entirely from "here."

Another thread in these poems is how the movement and mixing of ideas, like the butterfly's continental movement, is necessary for the survival of our species. We rely on the ability of these ideas to transcend the borders and barriers of ideology and "foreignness."

But the most important aspect of these poems is that they share feelings, because emotion is one of the things that makes us human; it transcends the barriers of time, of language, and of place. Thus, this book is an invitation to feel—to move one's heart to a different spot.

So savor these poems with all your senses. Let these feelings and ideas pass the borders and barriers of your heart and mind. Allow them to mingle with your sense of where you're from and where you're going or of where you've been and of who you are.

If you closely listen to, no, *feel* these poems, if you attend to the fluttering of the pages and the gliding of the words, your soul will be nourished by human warmth. If you allow yourself to move in the shadows and reflections of each poet's ideas, you'll perceive some of the forces that bend the arc of the moral universe. Not only that, you'll also be able to share your feelings, contribute your ideas, and lend your strength to these forces.

In many ways, this book is about who we are, where we've been, and where we ought to be headed. This is our human journey.

Introduction

by Lisa Vihos

On September 29, 2018, a group of poets and friends came together at Mead Library in Sheboygan, Wisconsin to share poems on the theme of migration and immigration. The open mic reading was my annual contribution to 100 Thousand Poets for Change (100TPC), a worldwide movement I have participated in since its beginning in the spring of 2011.

In the summer of 2018, I was shaken by the news of children caged and separated from their parents at our southern border, the unceasing talk of a wall, and targeted deportations of Latinx neighbors in my very own Wisconsin community. For the first time, I felt that my offering for 100TPC needed a theme. I wanted to bring voices together to think about the fact that many of us have come from somewhere other than where we have landed. Humans have always moved, some out of necessity and some by force. Whatever currents have pushed people, they've always brought with them pieces of their past, as many of these poems testify.

I found inspiration in a song brought to my attention by my friend, Alexandra Guevara. The song *Movimiento* (Movement) is by Uruguayan singer-songwriter, Jorge Drexler. I put the song's refrain out to the community as part of the call to the open mic, inviting people to respond:

> Yo no soy de aquí / I'm not from here
> Pero tú tampoco / But you're not either
> De ningún lado del todo / From nowhere entirely
> De todos lados un poco / From everywhere a little

People of all ages shared original poems at the event. Throughout the reading, I kept saying, "We have to make a book of these poems." And I've learned if you say something enough, it will happen.

A week later, I joined forces with Dawn Hogue at Water's Edge Press. She was excited by the idea and we put out a call for submissions through our various poetry circles. The response was huge—we were so moved by what we read. We are honored to share these poems with you here.

by Dawn Hogue

This fall, a flock of common merganser ducks arrived in Sheboygan. They came from the far north—the Yukon or Alaska—to spend their winter on the Sheboygan River. These bold black and white ducks are hard to miss. Their bright orange feet and beaks are so unlike what we're used to, their cousins the mallards. The mallards are beautiful as well, but they're our ordinary. They are year-long residents, and we see them every day. So when the mergansers arrived, they brought something "new." Because of them, our neighborhood is more diverse, more interesting, and more beautiful.

I have a feeling these ducks don't care whether or not others think they belong here. The mergansers have traveled far to find open water, and they are lucky the river makes no judgments. They float apart from the geese and the mallards, but in all, they coexist peacefully, even tolerating the noisy gulls that screech overhead.

If only we could all be like the river—simply accepting, we would find that being open to everyone never diminishes us.

These days, too many people put their arms over their chests and scowl at an old, false narrative: *all these immigrant people will hurt us*. The poems in this book tell a different story, a true story.

Wherever they're from, new neighbors bring diversity. They help us see the world in new ways and broaden our lives that would otherwise remain small. They also bring their stories, and if we're open to listening, we just may discover common threads: stories of leaving and arriving, of advice and prayer, of seeds and wings.

If only we could all be like the river—simply accepting, we would find that people are not so different after all. We all come *from everywhere a little*.

About 100 Thousand Poets for Change

100 Thousand Poets for Change was founded by Michael Rothenberg and Terri Carrion in Northern California in the spring of 2011. The two put out a call via Facebook to poets and musicians all over the world, inviting them to organize community poetry events on the final Saturday of September that would promote peace, justice, and sustainability. Every September since that time, 100TPC has happened not only in Sheboygan, Wisconsin, but in more than 300 cities all over the USA and the world. For more information about this amazing worldwide collective that continues to grow, visit www.100tpc.org.

From the Reading

100 Thousand Poets for Change
September 29, 2018
Sheboygan, Wisconsin

New Arrivals: 1980

face each other
i am 23 they 13
eyes are language
i arrive by college and car
they come from the war
tigers
green jungle
mountains
rivers tearing families
still crying
i point and say door
clock
chair
desk
my name
eyes of wonder
Mai Lee
Kong
Tai
draw pictures for me
November we talk
they teach me *Nyob Zoo*
Xyoo Tshiab
as an invitation
hand me a whole warm egg
welcome to the new year

United in Dream

Sing!
Sing the song of birds
that wrested you from slumber,
from aching feet,
following animals for food,
from those tired arms which carried
your child in dream state.

Be the dream state!
Praise and fear the mountains you travel.
Glory in the miles of savannah you tread.
Imagine in your mind the birth
of crops, of sustenance, of life
ongoing for family.

We are united in these wishes:
yours from the south of our earth,
mine from the northeast,
from a different sea to cross,
from a different route to take,
but with the same mindset,
the same lyric of hope.

The immigrant luggage we hoist is heavy.
Our families know that burden.
We share that journey.

Sing the troubles.
Sing the trials.
Sing the sickness.
Cry the infant, buried at sea.
Then listen again.

Listen to the survivors of the wind
and the currents and the wars.

We are united as genetic travelers
on that water droplet,
on that rock of ages, that meteorite.

We seek the vapor of life, oxygen.
Our cattle know the barriers.
They stretch their noses beyond fences.
They forever seek the sweet grass,
always beyond their grasp.

We could learn from our animals,
but here is the difference between us:
We dream for more than sustenance of body.
We see, not grass, but a river
and dream about the other side.
We know no barriers.
We dream for more than we can touch.
Our dream unites us.
We are the dream.

A Part of the Dawn

Picture yourself as a part of the dawn
gazing, as the morning comes, with your eyes,
look out there and tell yourself to go on

Science helps explain the phenomenon
and time in space we all visualize,
Picture yourself as a part of the dawn

Men and women all walk across a lawn
up to the houses to say their goodbyes,
Look out there and tell yourself to go on

Tomorrow, many of them will be gone
exploring the frontiers among the skies,
Picture yourself as a part of the dawn

Because of those travellers rolling on
you dream of your space race, when your ship flies,
Look out there and tell yourself to go on

Durable boots and clothes made of nylon,
Stand on the mountain and look at the skies,
Picture yourself as a part of the dawn
Look out there and tell yourself to go on

Hummus and Hot Dogs

when he crosses the bridge
wave at him
better still meet him
in the middle
where the common ground
of your footsteps
will lead both of you
to new land
where no one is foreign
and home
has many rooms
in the kitchen corner
the dictionary scratches out
alien, illegal, stranger
the stove cooks up
hummus and hot dogs
(bratwurst on Thursdays)

Lullaby for Troubled Times

Forget this world, its disrepair.
Forget the poisoned land and air.
Forget the stranded polar bear.
Sleep, baby, sleep.

Forget how sea will overflow.
Forget the bleaching reef below.
Forget the giant garbage floe.
Sleep, baby, sleep.

Forget the hunger greed can't quell.
Forget the dizzy carousel
of toys and games they try to sell.
Sleep, baby, sleep.

Forget the sick of heart and head.
Forget the guns they love instead.
Forget the hate that hate has bred.
Sleep, baby, sleep.

Forget the insults you will hear.
Forget the need to persevere.
Forget that they don't want you here.
Sleep, baby, sleep.

Forget the left, forget the right.
Forget the laws they will rewrite
while many suffer out of spite.
Sleep, baby, sleep.

Forget the wars you didn't choose.
Forget the children they abuse.
Forget the life you stand to lose.
Sleep, baby, sleep.

Forget the bombs that might be dropped,
each power play they try to top.
Forget the end that can't be stopped.
Sleep, baby, sleep.

Sleep with progress. Science too.
Diplomacy. The Golden Rule.
Dream of all the good you'd do.
Sleep, baby, sleep.

Immigrant Poem

I   miss my Dad
M exico is too far away
M isunderstood
I   will never stop fighting
G ot milk? Not without immigrants
R efugees are welcome here
A nti-racism
N ot seen you in six years
T rying hard to get you back

Fools

From nowhere at all,
From everywhere a little.
Fools.
We are fools.

We want the best, but expect the worst.
We believe others will come along
and make everything go smoother.

We want others to do things for us,
but complain when we grow tired of their ways.

We say we are free, but there are millions
who don't know what that means.
Child slavery, human trafficking,
and poverty do not go away.

Innocent until proven guilty
you make sure the truth is twisted
into lies so you won't be compromised.
It's all the same.

We are fools expecting things to get better
without any work, and yet complain
about the work of those who do.

Our country was founded by immigrants,
millions inspired to a better life.

Our streets are paved with gold,
and people are not persecuted in the night.
Our flag stands firm, the Statue stays tall.
And we are the fools mixed with them all.

Why Do We Have to Have a Seating Chart?

Because structure breeds creation
because this city is segregated
because you don't live near her
because she goes to her synagogue once a week
because you don't speak her language
because poverty speaks its own language

because this may be your last chance
because she smiles when she's nervous
because she can draw
because she is organized
because she may organize you

because you thought gypsy swing violin
because notes fly free
because notes on a page

because we came from somewhere else
we were down and out
because Hip Hop came from the South Bronx

because we dream
because we rise up
because we sit down
because we take a knee

because we pledge together
we pledge One Nation

The Voyage

1.
Maple leaves snap like sails
unfurling in a crowd of gusts.

Earth and all her inhabitants,
her elements, is about to set sail.

As sunset smolders through
treetop masts, I realize I've been

pressed into service. There's
no turning back.

Farewell, my predictable
landlubber life!

You've been a soothing illusion
for decades.

2.
Before long, we're becalmed.

The absence of wind and rain
shuts us in with noxious odors.

Toxic fumes infiltrate our lungs.
Many gasp for breath.

This is nothing like the home
of my youth.

We travel together on a ship so vast
its lower decks can never be plumbed.

There's no end to misery here.

3.
Consciousness of owning a stake
in conserving resources came too late
for most, who blocked all awareness
that the ship's stores could run out.

Now we realize we should have cut
our rations in half ages ago,
then halved them again, and again.

4.
Our Captain hungers for mêlée,
feeds on danger and drama.

Sometimes on Frigate Earth we
run out the big guns, practice
firing at targets.

I've decided to sit this skirmish out,
conceal myself belowdecks,
conspire with others to expose
and eradicate Tyranny, all its guises,
its falsehoods.

In fact, for the good of Frigate Earth,
I'm decidedly mutinous.

5.
Bravado aside, I believe the scientists
who predict this voyage will end badly,

that our captain, officers, wealthy passengers
will abandon Frigate Earth like rats,
relocate to another planet before most of us
figure out we're sinking.

Earth has been a beautiful experiment
doomed from the start by the behavior
of humans, our greed, shortsightedness,
violence.

We command the planet—and act as if
we want to destroy it.

Our current leaders take full advantage—
exploiting, despoiling, not giving back.

(Continues on next page)

6.
Suddenly a ferocious gust shakes us, heaves
Frigate Earth though turbulent swells.

Exhilaration turns to terror that the wind's
escalating tantrum will shred our vessel
and everything in it.

We cling to splinters of youthful delusions.
We strain to believe the captain's deceptions.

7.
I wish I could report that Frigate Earth
weathers the storm without
significant damage, but she does not.

The main mast has broken in half,
statecraft walked the plank,
Democracy is on the rocks.

It's up to us to free and repair the ship
before it breaks apart, fight for
the continued existence of Earth.

We're all in the same boat.
We depend on one another for survival.

Citizen of the World

for Anthony

Welcome, citizen of Chile, chileno nuevo.

Born in the land of Allende,
open your virgin eyes wide
to view the land that inspired Mistral and Neruda
and be inspired to do great things.

Welcome, American citizen, new American.

Open your ears to listen to the poetry of Whitman and Ferlinghetti
and hear what America should be, could be.

Born in the land of Pinochet,
open your eager mind to learn the history of your countries
and how they are connected;
learn the bloody history of the continents united in your blood.

Welcome, citizen of the world, human being.

Born in the New World, into the infancy of the next new world,
open your young heart and feel the love of your mother and your father.
Look them over closely and see that flags and borders can be meaningless.

Carry their love inside of you
and with that love, and their mixed blood,
inspire others, like your arrival inspires your family.

Oh, the great things you will see in your lifetime!

You

Show me
I want to see
I want to understand who you are,
where you came from

Tell me your stories from across the seas
from below the border, from desert cities
where sands blow like storms, from busy
markets filled with shouts and greetings
spoken in languages that taste of spices
and chocolate

Tell me the bad, the terrible
that brought you here, tell me about
the desert blown apart with explosions
houses crumbling to dust as light fades
the market blasted with gunshots
people dropped to the ground
with screams
And pleas of desperation

Tell me your desperate plea,
the hope and sorrow you felt
boarding that boat, crossing that fence,
tell me about your first footsteps
in the golden land of opportunity

Tell me how you were met with hatred
and scorn from this land of immigrants
where the color of your skin now equals
the worth of your soul

To survive you give in to the flow
Your words taste of sour and coal
You trade culture for job, home, clothes
You are afraid to be who you are

Tell me your stories in whispers
Let them be carried away
Let them seek out the other whispered words
Until the whispers become a voice, become a scream

Because *you*
who crossed oceans, crossed borders, crossed cultures
You are the best of us

Let *me* tell *you*
The immigrants, the outsiders, the refugees
All of you othered by America's broken,
backwards self-righteous regime
You are the ones
Making America Great Again

Cross Copulation

Cross Copulation
coupled with
Migration
creates a Diverse nation
One which
Everyone
should have a place in
Yet
based on the color of your face
Skin
that's still not always the case

See
there should be a
War
that rages inside of me
based on our sparring society
As I was born with
More Than One Race
that resides in me.
And not one of them can be
Erased

Yes
from all over the world
My Ancestors came
the Irish,
the Africans
the Brits,
the Bahamians
Through Hardships and Challenges
Some of which
Still Remain
though they'd HOPEd we'd be rid of them
they still get replayed
and still
THEY remain
bearing witness right here in my
Mixed DNA

That even though the road to
Our Freedom
still needs to be paved
we have grown and evolved
And have come a long way

And when you think of it all
at the end of the day
We are all
Very Much
the SAME

Beware of Bees During High Wind

Dedicated to Queen Lili'uokalani

Nu'uanu Pali was created for another day.
Gales of fog gust the lot of us;
Unless we fight it, we are almost away.
Along the path, from the limbering barks
So many drips damping us down.
Above, their crowning thrashes bewitched.
Achieving the cliff, huddled by a stone restraint,
What is there to see? Nothing--
The fog so thick it is a blind on the eyes,
A gag in the throat. And then,
And then the blind begins to lift,
As if there are ghosts who hold us hostage,
Gift a sight of their paradise to drive us mad,
Before they throw us over.
Mists thin to a veil which drifts discarded.
We view the molting mountainsides,
Inhabited hills. Beyond, but nigh,
An ocean wedded to its sky, so high.
It is a vision redenied. Once again,
The vista goes opaque and is lost.
"Intruder." Spoken by ghosts?
Or do I name myself.

At our feet, as if in another world,
A rooster and hen strut amidst bees,
Their chicks searching for feed.
Lively, they lighten the mood.
Perhaps, remembering, the ghosts desist.
In charity, they grant to each of us a clarity.
One sees the honey of a prize as simply this:
The stroll along a golden shore which curves
And curves, until it is a circle and complete.
Another wants to carve a magical rune
Into a candle; then, sit, and smell
The melting beeswax scent the night.
And I, to what do I aspire?
Witness. I see the generations,
Each, a hexagonal vessel for stories,
Histories which form an island hive, Hawaii.

Who will guard this legacy of kings?
Queen Lili'uokalani sang the answer.
Brother, sister traveler, become an oracle,
Divine the queen's soul.
Depart, but sing "Aloha Oe" to honor its composer,
Heed the sign: "Beware of BEES." Be fierce.

Leaving and Arriving

Papa's Lullaby

separation at the border

pobrecito, niño mío
you're alone and the night is so long
it's the reason I give you this song
you must be strong

hear the music from abuela's garden
there is nothing can keep us apart
know your papa he loves you
and holds you deep in his heart

pobrecito, you can sleep now
close your eyes   here's a kiss maybe two
no importa whatever they do
I am with you

hear the music from abuela's garden
there is nothing can keep us apart
know your papa he loves you
and holds you deep in his heart

when your sandals are under the bed
hug your pillow and lay down your head

Sunday Lunch in Exile

We didn't talk about our suffering
We taught our children patience
Mastering the silent endurance
Our masters said:
Unnecessary sorrows hijack the glory of God
So, we ate the crumbs from their table
without any complaint.
We comforted ourselves : *I'm fine. It's ok.*
Tomorrow will be the same,
The concept of discrimination repeats itself.
Gentlemen from social institutions will remind me again
that I'm just a number in the system.
I will be thinking again
how I should leave everything.
Maybe move to another city, another country.
I comforted myself with the illusion of love,
understanding, and forgetfulness
But deep in my heart I knew.
There is no country for immigrants.

Gao Xingjian leaves Beijing

returns to his village
carrying a fishing rod for his grandfather.
The gate to his house that guarded 28 generations
is gone, the house is gone, his grandfather is gone,
the river that ran through the village is gone. He finds
a dry concrete ditch, finds a mountain gouged by machines,
finds a sky tangled with wires and telephone poles, sees strangers
who gawk at him, wanders without bearings, without fish,
only the ditch, the concrete, the wires,
the dust, the faces of strangers.

Inspired by Gao Xingjian, Buying a Fishing Rod for My Grandfather: Stories, 1984, 2004.

When You Left

Did you foresee,
Generations later—
Your son, Your grandson, Me
Walking into your preserved church,
Sitting in the wooden pew,
Listening to sermons
¿En tu idioma?

Did you believe
Your atoms could
Carve crevices into Andes,
Absorb Caribbean ardor,
Escape
Suicides, deserts,
Entreat
Vineyards, mountains,
Encounter
Siestas,
        Morcilla
¿Boinas,
Pañuelos,
Violines,
Llantos?

On your final gaze
Upon red-green hills,
Golden under sunset,
And fertile rivers,
Turbulent under shadow,
Did you imagine
A little boy
Arriving
In a barren man's body,
Lifting
A pebble in your honor?
Demanding
More wine!
More life!
¿En tus calles?

Memory shivers in old gray walls—
Energy worming through time.

The Immigrant

Stoically shook Father's hand,
awkwardly embraced Mother,
boarded the train bound for Helsinki
and the boat.
Seventeen, on his way to America,
never to return,
or speak to his parents again.
Ship mail was slow, but they would write.

Minnesota held forests and lakes,
reminders of home.
Offered work on railroads
and lumber camps.
In his suitcase were some clothes,
a few photographs,
courage and determination.
He carried dreams by the handle.

Opportunity

Jose's parents bend, cut, toss cabbages,
rummaged clothes a shield in unflinching sun.
They cup Jose's cherubic face, review their rules,
tighten their embrace before the long ride to find work,
limp, as the pulsing lights of La Migra reflect off the gas pump.

Eight-year-old Jose obeys, stays in the flat
until his neighbor, now legal, drives him to school,
where curiosity's tinder is ignited with Lewis and Clark,
volcanoes of vinegar, field trips to Black Creek Library,
practice seats at the Timber Rattlers.

Jose, unattended after school, large book in a little lap,
pries open mathematical problems like sweet tangerines,
grasps the scientific, pours over the worldly, believes.
No cell phone, no Xbox, no video games,
but an eager heir, alone in a land of opportunity.

Intransitives Need No Object

Elsa has a past full of color
and some mystery I do not pursue.
My task is to teach her English
not quiz her on personal history.

But vocabulary is like a prompt
for a poem she is writing to keep
memories of family and home.

    Fill in the blank with a linking verb
    like *tastes* or *smells*:
    This honey *(tastes)* wonderful.

But for Elsa the *honey (was) wonderful...*
in stories she tells about her beekeeping aunt.

    Sticky combs *taste* wonderful.
    Buzzing *sounds* wonderful.
    Flowers *smell* wonderful,
    The sun *feels* wonderful.

On Monday afternoons at the kitchen table
Elsa reveals her *historia* one word at a time.

I Went With My Brother

I went with my brother
to see the old clapboard
he bought
in the hilly country and
standing there, feeling our
history—cousins cracked, parents
dead, dairy cows too, our divorces,
the kids grown up—I looked

at cornstalks rimming the hills
a kind of light between
honey and butter and behind us

his new place to live
with outbuildings, a shed
maybe I'll get some chickens
he said
a kind of peace
a kind of coming home

Journey

At Somerset and Buncombe and Danville
the train stops, collects the shabby
standing with cardboard grips, buttoned-up
faces—I see this in sepia now—Kentucky
of 1940 slipping along our windows: snow-
dusted hills, bronze-leafed woods, fields
abandoned by red-knuckled farmers gone in

to wood fires and newspapers rattling of
far-off war, while November's brown mouth
swallows track as we leave it, inhales our
engine's steam, and we become a long noise
rattling our way on a workers' pilgrimage,
past the make-believe of Lexington, Daddy
pointing to white fences, silk-sleek horses,

Mother turning from the baby to the splendid
houses, the sun streaming its gold around us,
a sign I believe—we're going to get rich—
but nightfall erases all, releases stale air,
the window becomes mirror-hazed,
disembodied faces in passing trains, babies
crying, until at last Daddy says "It's the river"

and takes me on his knee to see the bridge,
so long a crossing, soft sheen on black water,
then the lights—lights stunning and flashing,
puncturing the high bank of darkness, dabs of
sparkle rising to a fixed restlessness, merging
into a luminous pall: Ohio, the next galaxy.

In My Mother's Recipe Box

In a cloud of flour you will find
my Great-Grandmother Marie, Aunt Minnie,
Grandma Mimi, and my mother.
Meet them on three by fives filed in a flip-top wooden box.
Well-thumbed tabs expel paper dust,
bent edges divide tastes of the past
into breads, cookies, desserts, meats, vegetables.

In my mother's recipe box you will find
slant-cursive writing in blue fountain pen,
ingredient lists, directions and temperatures continued on the backs.
In my mother's recipe box touch Aunt Minnie's dough
smudges on *Sugar Cookie Cut Outs*, and
her gravy stain on our beloved *Norwegian Meatballs*.

In my mother's recipe box see chocolate prints on a family
favorite, *Chocolate Brownies*, initials "MHB" in the corner,
still oven-warm, shiny on top, moist in the middle.
In my mother's recipe box try Grandma Mimi's
light *Lemon Cookies* served at tea time and
her flaky pie crust rolled with the one-handled rolling pin.

My mother's recipe box holds the imprint of strong women
who rolled potato dough for *Lefse*.
Great-Grandma Marie's strong hands kneaded *Yulekake*,
cardamom-citron Christmas bread, dough that
stretched across four generations and one wide ocean,
escaping scarcity, bringing recipes,
seeking abundance, rising in a new land.

Home

I don't remember my mother
teaching me anything
about being Persian.
She didn't introduce me
to our foods, our tongue,
our traditions.
I don't remember her
drinking tea after meals
or cooking stew for days.

By the time I was ten,
I had only my grandfather,
who believed Farsi
would not be useful
and being American
was important.
He would try to make
American food
for me and my sisters,

But I always preferred
the deep amber chay
that Persians drink,
the taste of feta with
cherry jam on sangak
that Persians eat,
the rugs and rich stews
and big families
that Persians have.

My grandfather
could not predict the way
I would crave his past,
the things he could only
associate with pain,

like home.

The Hole

1.

When the Black Hand shot
Archduke Franz Ferdinand in the jugular
on a bridge in Sarajevo near her village,
Branca was six. She had been taught
the *goyim* would beat her with a cross
if she entered the forest.

As that shot started World War I,
her father—to her a faded photo
on her mama's farmhouse wall—
got a message through.
He'd found a place for them
in New York City, America.
You must come now.

2.

On Delancey Street, Branca's teacher
poked her sharp-nailed finger
through her pink angora sweater.
What's this hole, Jewgirl?
She yanked the threads, gave Branca
a shiksa name: Betty—

I had to quit school because we couldn't afford
a gym suit, Mother told me
when I was old enough to understand.
I was a beauty, too smart for my own good.
I buried myself in books and boys and men,
and then, your father.

The hole grew larger.

3.

Mother sang show tunes with the radio.
Outside our third floor window,
a dark shaftway rang with davening.
Across the alley in the shul's
sparse square of dirt,
weeds and garbage grew.

She dressed me in pinafores,
checkered coats with velvet collars from B. Altman's.
Hand in hand we'd walk the wooden floors,
peering into showcases. She picked dresses,
pointed out wide pleated sleeves looked like accordions.
Smooth silk sashes, yards of petticoats,
for her to press away creases.

I dressed and undressed my bride doll,
sent by Dad from somewhere far away,
while Mom tried on clothes in the open dressing room.
Olive-pupiled eyes opened and shut.
Click-click, click-click.

4.

I learned to sing her favorite songs
so we could harmonize.
Much later, I paid for lipsticks she pocketed
from Woolworth's five and dime.

Rudy Vallee almost discovered me,
Mother told me many times—
We were crossing Fifth Avenue.
He came right up, said I should be in movies
because I'm gorgeous. Rudy Vallee! And your father
just kept yanking me across the street.

Mit Patience

for San Antonio

My grandmother once told me it was these—
The cabbage and the cherry—they missed most
When her family emigrated here from

Germany. But cabbages and cherries
Grew here too, once they planted them. Small ghosts
Of the past clung to the new leaves, lonesome

At first, stubbornly remaining as Kirsch
Strudel, Krautkuchen, Kalt Rotkohl before
Stretching out in New World permutations.

Cornbread-Cabbage, Curtido, Prickly Pear
Cherry Upside Down Cake. *See, they transfer
Well,* my grandmother would say, *Für sicher,*

A Dr. Pepper in hand, *mit patience
Things come together,* as she put cayenne
On cole slaw, cherries on a Leche-Flan.

Letter to My Great-Grandmother, RE: Her Luck

At the wedding, the priest writes *female of doubtful
reputation* in the record. The baby, a girl,
dies of measles. You and the husband,
ten years younger, flee to Yonkers,
live in the lint of a carpet factory.
The loom yawns and jaws
open every dream. You pick
wool fibers out of the soup,
the water pitcher; they form a fine
webbing at the bottom of the Mason jar.
The jar-money buys the farm, the biggest
orchard in your old village, for the son. O gift
of the unexpected son! You migrate home triumphant,
arrive just in time for German shells to crack the new ceiling.

Advice and Prayers

Refugees

We came with heavy suitcases
made from wooden boards by brothers
we left behind, came from Buchenwald
and Katowice and before that
Lwow, our mother's true home,

came with our tongues
in tatters, our teeth in our pockets,
hugging only ourselves, our bodies
stiff like frightened ostriches.

We were the children in ragged wool
who shuffled in line to eat or pray
or beg anyone for charity.

Remembering the air and the trees,
the sky above the Polish fields,
we dreamt only of the lives waiting
for us in Chicago and St. Louis
and Superior, Wisconsin

like pennies
in our mouths.

The Promise

The wind shifts the smoke
southward like winter birds
over neighboring towns I was raised
to hate for reasons even my father
can't remember, over horses
and wilder dogs, empty silos, broken
fences, hills stripped of coal, long
stretches of placelessness; then farther
and farther to villages no longer starred
on maps and cities the movies
depict as beautiful violences,
neon-lit and sleepless; finally
skimming across open oceans
like hard-thrown stones to where
people look up to us as beacons
of light, praying so fiercely with all
their bodies for a chance to breathe
what I cannot clear from my lungs.

Driving Without a License

Stay away from rich suburbs,
especially at night. Never wear
a hat that makes you look
especially Mexican. Try to have
a child in the car with you, or
better, a gringo, well dressed,
blonde if possible. Always
wear your seat belt. Check
your taillights every hour
or so, and make sure no one
is out. Signal carefully.
Turn down the music, or turn
on country. Never take your
phone out, or your name out,
or your country. Or your fear.
I know you want a Virgen
or a Santito on the dash,
but they work just as well
tucked inside your glove box.

Refugees

We think we have left the enemy behind
but even when we no longer live in the camps,
(temporary, but long enough for several seasons
of crops to ripen on our small plot of land,
long enough for some to open little businesses,
cafes)

even after we've answered questions
over and over and put our names
on official papers: yes this is true, yes
they did that to us, yes these are my brothers,
my sisters (well really the daughters
of my father's second wife)

even when we've landed with our bundles
in a place where we don't understand
the language, and moved into an apartment

we are afraid. Even then,
out of the corner of an eye,
we see them. They are always there.

Advice for Travelers

When you leave your country, put your papers
    in a plastic bag, then zip it shut.
When you leave your country, hide money
    in your shoe or in your underpants.
When you leave, put crackers in your pocket
    and an extra shoelace too.
And you better know how to swim and be ready
    to walk all day.
Learn to say "when" and "why." Learn how to move
    your tongue. Learn how to shape your lips.
Remember a blanket when you leave,
    for nowhere will be soft.
When you leave your country, your thoughts will
    sift like flour through a sieve. And when
you leave your country, your name may curl
    inside your ribs and tap like insects
    on a windowpane at night.
Leave your country and you'll find rooms and streets
    of children, but they may not be your own.
When you leave, you may study your open palm
    and wonder if your future's hiding there.
When you leave, you may lose your
    body and then what becomes of you?
Leave, and you may find that no one tells the truth
    and truth is sitting on a chair that wobbles on three legs.
And even after you leave, your country's hard
    and stubborn, a tiny seed stuck
    between your teeth
And you can't tell if the taste is bitter or if
    you're tasting something sweet.

Phoenix

If you were like me
you'd understand
why chicken and
kitchen
are so alike
or
he and
she
for that matter.
You laugh at me
and I think of

all the silly mistakes you would make if you were me.
I give you
a lifetime.
Say ققنوس
(and good luck!)
whenever you are ready.
Then we go flying together,
as the birds
laugh at our accents.

Postcard from Ikuno

I thought it was an earthquake
awakening me.
The bed shook,
dream over?

It was only workmen
blasting a tunnel through the mountain
just beyond the river.

Later that morning, my first visit
to a Japanese market,
I gazed at a shrink-wrapped squid.

That one glazed eye. The heavy metal
stereo flaring storewide.

My new life in Japan,
my guidebooks useless.

If Only Caetano Veloso Knew He Was Singing to Me

with his soft, tenor voice
could be calling me linda

asking me to look at time
passing outside the window.

When he says I've left him
alone for so long that he might

be tempted to look elsewhere for love,
I understand.

Decades ago, I left.
Only been back once.

Didn't even tell him.
I wanted to see him

when he came to Miami
but I had a work thing.

When he cries, "você não me ensinou
a te esquecer" the truth is I can't teach

something I've never learned.
And in my breakup letter, I'll confess

I'm afraid of love, of men,
of what we would do with all the singing.

Prayer Beads

Long bead strand
wraps her wrist.
Not a rosary
no suffering Jesus
dangles on the end.
Like a rosary
she clicks each bead.

As our plane
runs through rain clouds,
jostles us like laundry
on the spin cycle,
her prayers and mine
keep the plane aloft.

The man across the aisle
asks the flight attendant
to make her stop.
Her noise bothers him.

She gently complies,
but I hope her prayers continue.
I can't keep the plane up
all by myself.

Skein

> When giving the signal to his birds, they arose in the air with him for their journey to the moon. —Francis Godwin, "The Strange Voyage of Domingo Gonsales to the World in the Moon."

Hours after class, in my office,
I meet with a student I haven't seen
in over three weeks, wondering where she's been.
She tells me she hasn't come to class because
she's afraid for her parents.
They came from El Salvador. Saved
their money to get across
the border, paid the coyotes, couldn't bring
everyone, only the clothes on their backs
and one small bag that carried
a photo of the family, all of them
together, the last time.

This was before she was born, before
she was the fleck of gold in their eyes.

She shows me the photo on her phone. Faces
smiling through a Polaroid-orange haze.
Her eyes glossy with tears, *that's my tia and my
grandmother and grandfather*, people she
has never met.

My parents aren't safe here now, she tells me,
I'm afraid they will get caught.
Black-wet mascara makes a trail
down her face, *I wish I could carry them
to someplace safe, the moon
maybe*, she says and laughs, wipes her cheeks on her jacket sleeves,
zips her backpack—leaves—but not before promising to
turn in the missing work.

I believe she will, and then I'm left
alone in my office where I think about
an essay, a tall-tale really,
read in a long-ago linguistics class
about a man who, aided by two dozen
harnessed geese in their migratory pattern,
flew to the moon, and I imagine my student, her parents,
and a skein of geese, silent, as they are lifted up through the silvery clouds.

Truth of the Mayan

The Mayans didn't disappear
into a shroud of cloud one mystical day—

Broken and spent from centuries of
erecting monuments
climbing ziggurats
listening to potent tongues
betray them
finally fled the jaws of imperialists
to hide pulsing hearts
brawny backs
gold in their teeth

Protected by night
taking nothing but bones
stole to the uncivilized hills
seeking lost souls

Here, the people heard parrots sing
took food from willing trees
found spirits waiting to weave
prisms into warm, woolens
for hundreds of years
and still do—
but, now
look over their shoulders
toward the roar of the Caterpillar
closing in at a steady pace
and this time
there's nowhere left to go—

Dobrze (well)

Because we come from everything:

My grandmother (busia) escaped Poland before World War I as a teenage girl of sixteen. Sadly, her parents had to stay behind. She spoke Polish first, but later (when I was a young child) she was bilingual. I remember her speaking only Polish with old Mr. Printke from down the street. My parents could also speak both, but later when I was older (five? six?) I recall only English.

Now, Lynn and I are in Poland and the Poles are worried, again. KGB relic Putin shirtless, riding a horse, scoring every goal in a hockey game, and winning the popular vote at ninety-four percent. Russia back to the U.S.S.R. Poland didn't even exist for one hundred and twenty-three years. Other times in its history, shrinking and expanding borders like Silly Putty.

Krakow's Old Town on a warm July evening, full Polish moon. Violins, accordion music, outdoor dining, people floating over the cobblestones. We check out the shops (amber from the Baltic Sea, the cloth market). Saint Wojciech church. There is only one drunk sitting against a wall, with his upturned hat shouting, "I need kawa!"

In the Polish restaurant, walk in the door to be greeted by the host with a tray of shot glasses filled with vodka. "Dziekuje," I say, and head for the food. On the small dance floor, the polka dancers skip and hop and we join them for a dance or two. On the table: pierogis, kielbasa, kapusta, szefser, potato pancakes.

In the un-united states, an orange man has ordered fifteen thousand troops to deploy, not in the decades-old war, but along, "THE WALL," to protect fearful (mostly white folks) from the invasion. "They're bad hombres, they're rapists, they're murderers! There are caravans…" I ask, "Who will clean your hotels? Who will milk your cows? Who will pick your fruit?" The horror of Honduras, the old "banana republic" still alive, but not well.

Driving through the Tetra Mountains, rich green, but now a torrent of rain. In the countryside the Polish flats, houses raised up with quarters for in-laws below. Chickens like in old vibrant Milwaukee and Chicago and gardens to show. In the morning we are heading for Warsaw where I pray that the press is not
"the enemy of the people" or too slow.

Tribal Identity

When she speaks, worry-lines fine as
cornsilk frame my neighbor's fjord-blue
eyes. *I don't see color. I just see people.*

> She means well, but judgement's bred
> into our bones, piggybacked on
> on lullabies, nursery rhymes, folktales
> heard in the cradle.

Camouflaged by my husband's French
surname, I pose no threat, blend into crowds.
The country I once called home
colored my heart,

> but not my face. My speech harbors
> no trace of another language.
> My Mexican-American son
> carries his U.S. passport as a shield.

With Asian features, cinnamon skin,
his doll-sized wife draws furtive glances,
crass questions, despite her Minnesotan lilt.

> I'm guilty too—I flip to the chapbook's
> back page, gaze at the poet's photograph,
> scan the blurb in search of her tribal identity.

An Iraqi-American, she threads Arabic
script through English text—filigree
pinned to plain cotton. Writes
of her father murdered in Baghdad,

> brother tortured in prison, mother
> unhinged by loss. Panic attacks
> on the Fourth of July.
> How to grow up in exile.

What she feels when strangers
brand her "terrorist" because she
wears a hijab.

Home is Elsewhere

Home, overnight, you are a step into the blind. A crammed safety-raft on choppy seas. A neighborhood in Noah's canoe. A toddler wrapped in fleece blankets. Infant food in plastic pouches tucked into blouses. You are the fleeing, the landing, the reaching. A reluctant ribbon of earth.
Land under swollen-raisin feet.

You are survivor bread wrapped in parachute nylon. Mildew and mold. In our skyward gaze, you are the cedars, the gumtrees, the open-beaked sunbird in a mangled nest. Padlocked songs of nightingales. Voiceless crayons rolling on tiles. And in the twilight hour, you are the serrated symmetry of sky against broken parapets.

You are submerged crypts of stars that predicted good fates. The satire. Tightly sewn skin of silence over cult. Visceral visions of hot toast and butter, cheese and brandy. Black coffee sipped on low wooden stools. The camaraderie of bi-lingual conversations across low boundary walls.

At the three a.m. hour, you are a vase, a door handle, fan blades, a secret hairpiece hooked behind an attic door, sheep in the pen, arms to long for, the lost compass, the hysteria that bursts forth from the aporia of taking the step into the blind.

In this camp of gashed fingers, brave faces, beggar hands, tear motifs, cold water through cheap taps, windy tents framing windows to a zilch destiny, Godlike violations of hope velcroed to hunted-deer eyes, fresh fresh gravestones. . . . You are a boldness that we dare to dream of.

First Day of School

We already know
cutting sheds and field work
better than some
fully grown men.

We are born afraid to fail,
clutch job lists
written by mama,
responsibility hard-coded
in stubborn wrinkles of brain.

On that first day of school,
we stack our
salami-scented lunch sacks,
trade family dialect
for English only
and chunky crayons.

At recess, while town kids
recite movie stars' names
and sing top 40 hits,
we think about
starting dinner,
getting the family ironing done.

In class,
we are the nervous ones,
sitting behind an invisible line,
one foot on the floor,
worried sick,
getting ready to run.

Seeds and Wings

Sandhill Cranes along the Platte River

Into the mutable colors of dusk, bugles of thousands
    wrest open the sky. Crisscross of flight after flight.
        A horizon of extended necks and stretched-out legs.

The gray shape-shifting mass dissolves, separates, and unites.
    Wings rattle the air, multitudes call back and forth—
        family to family, parent to child. They rend

and mend the skyways, trumpet choruses that bind like an invisible thread,
    millions of years stitching one generation to the next.
        Into the flap and flutter of deepening twilight

we follow the grand convocation, a spectacle of
    crimson crowns, tumultuous explosion of cries,
        wings flicking just slightly upward before

graceful, gangly legs drop down into courtships of bows and leaps,
    jumps and pirouettes. They throw back their heads, they bounce.
        The chicks imitate the acrobatic dance of parents. In awe

we watch skein upon skein of returning cranes come here to roost, to stand
    one-legged throughout the night, recreating the Platte and prairie
        into cranes as far as the eye can see.

The Iowa

It began at the bottom of a shallow sea.
Dried and flooded, a seabed, a wetland, a plain,
Home to a swimming, sucking, crawling, breathing
Darwinian daydream.

Its bedrock hardened in the Mississippian
and Devonian eras.
That's 300 million years to you and me.
And then came the glaciers.

Down a smooth carved contour
coursed the rains.
Washing geologic history toward the great river
breathless for a human footstep.

The peoples came with names like Winnebago,
Oto, Missouri, Omaha, Ponca, and Iowa.
Cultivators, a settled society,
easy on the rich lands, sated by the waters.

In those days, even the great waters ran clear.
But you know what happened.
The coming of the hard boot, the horseshoe,
the plowshare, barbed wire, and a gun.

The story ran down the watershed in muddy waters.
New names defined the landscape: ditch, trough, offal pit, sewer.
Pouring off organic beings, the flow of refuse—
Sloughing off the shuddering land, a great delta of topsoil.

Still we came, shat, tossed, spat
claimed the waters as a birthright.
And do not think that what you ate for dinner last night
is not part of this story.

Gypsy Steps

when I take leave
at dawn
the earth meets my pulse

the hills vibrate
underneath my soles
a giant snake breathing

then it comes to me
that all land
is attached

even when the sea splits it
it joins underwater
this ground I tread on

they can't chase me from earth
just ban me
from this or that town

a bit farther I'll step
on soil that still holds me

and it is the same one

Ode to Wild Fennel

Foeniculum Vulgare

Here's to you—worshipped by the ancients
to ward off evil spirits, restore lost vision,
for treatment of poisoning and infections,
for the kisses and weeping of women
on hands and knees
or lying next to you awhile
in open fields aflame with green,
consuming the tissue that sweetens breaths,
helps breast milk flow
always the healing herb in prayer and in fever.

Here's to your caned stems and lacy fronds
old as the bird, the wind, the migrant's shoes
that dispersed your anatomy of miracles
from the Mediterranean basin
to new sea cliffs, yard shrines, cracks
in the road, gravel driveways
of stately homes, and neighborhoods
brimming with crumbling foundations.
In a world where despair and disparity grow,
wild fennel, you sneak up on us like love.

My heart swells
you still appease the poor man's hunger,
trim appetites of the rich grown too fat,
take root by the graves of the dead
where human wars are over.
I wish I could be a charitable plant
with no sense of self importance,
no clever perspectives
drinking sunlight and filaments of rain,
assisting all sentient beings in need
but I'll say no more about that.
They prescribe medication
for this kind of talk in America—where I
struggle like hell to be merciful.
I could speak a well of anger
about new wars, border walls, and how
the clock is moving
between one breath and another for all of us.

But to see you is to see
free, unending life at work.
I can touch and taste —uninterrupted
life from before there were rooftops.
What gift to find you here beside a stone
among last year's brittle oak leaves
as the April night descends
and there's a bit of wind makes you tremble,
makes a baby rabbit up its ears and pose.
Everything else is quiet in Oysterponds.
Can you see me bend and bury my face
deep into your willowy leaves?
I'm so grateful for the green elegance,
won't even close my eyes, as in prayer.
All of me wide open and wake, inhaling
sweet licorice scent
for a moment of uncomplicated happiness.

Translating a Life

for O.M. and M.R.

Someone spread a blanket of wild buckwheat
over a meadow. Someone tucked puffball pillows
in each corner of the purple-green sheet.
It is summer everywhere, except war.
War, where it used to be home,
and now, war by government, here.
And what does it matter that the meadow
seduces the bees in pollen, or me in lines
of a poem, or that I hear perfectly good
Russian names for plants and translate them
into You-and-Me-ish? Take the tea mushroom,
the little fox mushrooms and piggies,
the early field-dweller, the mysterious
cheese-eater. These words don't have a visa
here, and the country that sent them erases
every syllable with its crimes.
Take an under-birch-mushroom
anyway—it's a choice edible,
birch bolete in your tongue, on
the tongue. The language for falling in love
with mushrooms, stories, or friends
does not care who's killing whom.
Unfortunately, I care. And, sitting here
by a huge flowering bush, I see no refuge.
What languaged fantasy could stop us
from being murderous strangers? Would you
take a Russian mushroom name,
tuck it in your lapel for the brief banquet of life?
Does that translate anything else for you?
Is this how it works?

Migration

Karen hates the spring time geese
that congregate around the pond,
ousting the mallards and the pie-billed grebes,
slender necks aloft, piqued S's,
vaguely regal: I imagine
indignant aristocrats flying whitely
from conjured threats. *They're dirty*,
she says, *bad for the land*, as if migration
were a matter of taste, free of the filth
demarking transit from one empire
to another, until there are no more
homes left to flee. I don't tell her
that I enjoy the chatter, the nasal croaking
of a gaggle combing the grass for grubs.
I like to think they sought us out,
the safest respite before taking flight
once more to v their way toward better
waters. I don't even mind that the yard
has been left mucky enough to stain
my bare feet when I stand in the centipede
grass, still as a cloud, watching the sky
for some new visitor.

Ornamental

The ornamental tree
      outside my bedroom window
      has clusters of red berries,
      though she is far from home.
A cutting from an imported seed,
      she hangs each cluster
      from a thin stem,
      tiny lanterns for my dreams.

What birds or animals
      ate her fruit
      in her native land?
      None eats it here.
Winters, when she is an etching
      of black and crimson on white,
      the cardinal sits in her branches
      to flaunt his brilliant breast,

but my dreams nibble
      her poison berries,
      to carry bits of Lethe
      into me
as I lie beneath red-lacquered lanterns
      to wander far
      from vinyl siding
      and darkened window pane.

Like a Raspberry Seed between my Teeth

Across the road
a white screen door slaps.
Redwing blackbirds scatter.

Cattails' slow explosions
fill the ditch.
I crack a beer and watch.

Last night at the Badger Tap
someone asked me why
I came back to Wisconsin.

Even in peacetime
ten years in the Navy
was killing me.

An east-to-west airliner
slowly flies over.
Its contrail spreads.

Sometimes it's what
we're not
that matters most.

Palm

Clenched in your hand:
Sorrow, or weight—
the things your selfishness makes you
 want to carry—
your life forces,
your unspoken words?

It is a matter of neither
flying nor drowning.
Just walking.
Walking, heavily weighted,
back loaded and strapped,
hands clenched full of either
treasures or refuse.

Fences crisscross the clear path
away from the storm front,
out of the ravaging winter.
If not, we would pour down the
landscape like loosed water,
and find a place, a place
to soak and settle,
to slowly curl open the palm
and look.

Wildlife Corridors

During the drought
I left a bowl of water
and scattered chicken
bones for the coyotes
in my back acreage
to slurp and crunch.

I know I'm not supposed
to invite the wild home.
Still, I feel protective
of underfed natives
eking a living
amidst concrete walls.

Treeline

The treeline has held its proud border
Since the glaciers receded,
Holding its ground
Where the cold is ageless
Where summer gets chills
Where few people venture.
But now treeline is moving
Migrating with the rest of us
On this profit-scorched Earth,
Heading for the hills
Losing our roots
Catching our breath
And crashing into a future no one wanted.

Where will the treeline go?
Down to the river
To drown lost and alone?

We are all wanderers again
But this time the weather
Wanders with us.

Migrations

The stealth of migrations
move across the land
under cover of darkness,
moving in hundreds
and then thousands.

You told me
about your car lights
shining in a canyon
one night—
"More elk than
one could imagine,"

moving to the southern places
where canyons lap over canyons,
lands whose vastness is greater
than the mind can comprehend,

unlike the northern deer
that migrate further north
to find giant spruce trees
whose branches touch
the ground to make
a snowless, warm canopy
for the wintering.

You said, "The axe blade
is sharpened, ready
to chop the bone
at the joints."

Monarch Butterflies

Sometime in fall the air tells them, milkweed
ages and their slight bodies concur—
it is time. Each day to find thermals, each
night to drop down, be still. They seem poorly

equipped for covering long distances,
flutter erratically, a sort of loopy,
bungling flight. Oyamel firs mean rest.
In their bed of nails one makes no sound we

can hear but in large numbers—a thrum of
life, whir of air moved by stained-glass-window
wings. Something like whispered chant. Millions
of tongues of flame, a thin, dry glossolalia. Oh,

when the whole congregation assembles
their muffled applause becomes a prayer
of earnest intent, a prayer for survival.
Christmas ornaments, Pentecostal flare—

they are part of something bright-beautiful,
something larger than what any one can
be. Some are coins new-minted, some are all
fade and tatter— tired as human migrants.

Year after year it happens   and still
we're oblivious. Lives different than our own,
whose inner need tells them, *Risk it all*.

White Birds

Canyon Pintado, Colorado

They soar
up a slant of sandstone
into the sky,

above all that is below—
the corn stalks that thrive
or that wither,

the creatures that slither
or crawl or walk,
the wind that sweeps

all things sideways,
the walls we build
against it—

two spirits rising
out of time
together (not alone).

About the Contributors

Vinita Agrawal is a Mumbai-based, award-winning poet. She has authored four books of poetry. Her work has been widely published and anthologized. She was judge for the RLFPA Awards (International category) in 2016. She is on the advisory board of The Tagore Prize.

Eneida Alcalde's poetry has been published or is forthcoming in literary outlets such as *The Chaffin Journal*, *Mad Swirl*, and *Boricua en la Luna: An Anthology of Puerto Rican Voices*. Her poem was inspired by a visit to her great-grandfather's hometown in La Rioja, Spain. Learn more about her at www.eneidapatricia.com.

Joe Amaral's first poetry collection *The Street Medic* won the 2018 Palooka Press Chapbook Contest. He works 48-hour shifts as a paramedic on the California central coast. His writing has appeared in *3Elements Review*, *Anti-Heroin Chic*, *New Verse News*, *Panoply*, *Poets Reading the News*, *Rise Up Review*, and elsewhere.

Nancy Austin has lived on both coasts, but prefers the Northwoods in between. Her works have appeared in *Adanna*, *Ariel*, *Gyroscope Review*, *Midwestern Gothic*, *Portage Magazine*, *Zingara Poetry Review*, and chapbooks titled *Remnants of Warmth* (Aldrich Press, 2016) and *The Turn of the Tiller; The Spill of the Wind* (Aldrich Press, forthcoming, 2019).

Mary Jo Balistreri is the author of three full-length books of poetry and a chapbook. She has been nominated for a Pushcart Prize and has received other awards as well. Most recently she placed first in two categories from the Illinois State Poetry Society. Latest publications are *Bards Against Hunger*, *Van Gogh Dreams*, and *Love Affairs from the Villa Nelle*. Please visit her at maryjobalistreripoet.com

Aileen Bassis is a visual artist in New York City working in book arts, printmaking, photography, and installation. Her artwork can be viewed at www.aileenbassis.com. She was awarded an artist residency in poetry to the Atlantic Center for the Arts. Her poems have appeared in *B o d y Literature*, *Spillway*, *Grey Sparrow Journal*, *Canary*, *Stone Canoe*, *The Pinch Journal*, and *Leveler*. She recently had two poems nominated for a Pushcart Prize.

Kaitlyn Becker was born in Kenosha, WI and began to write poetry at the age of seven. She is currently a high school student in Sheboygan and aspires to be a zoologist one day.

Rosalind Brenner, painter/poet, received her MFA in Poetry from Sarah Lawrence College. She's been published in *The Cortland Review*, *Poetry Bay*, *Taproot Journal*, *Ontologica*, *The Poetic Bond*, and *The Arroyo Literary Review*, among others. Rosalind's two books are *Omega's Garden* (Finishing Line Press) and *All That's Left* (Art House Press). Her forthcoming book from Blue Light Press is *Every Glittering Chimera*. Learn more about her art and poetry at rosalindbrenner.com.

James Burton is a high school teacher who is passionate about seeing and exploring the world. He enjoys writing as personal reflection and as a reflection of the people and places he interacts with in the world.

Originally from Pennsylvania, **Sylvia Cavanaugh** has an M.S. in Urban Planning. She teaches high school African and Asian cultural studies and advises break dancers and poets. A Pushcart Prize nominee, her poems have appeared in various publications. She is a contributing editor for *Verse-Virtual: An Online Community Journal of Poetry*. Her newest chapbook, *Angular Embrace*, was published by Kelsay Books in 2018.

Ethel Mortenson Davis has published five books of poetry. Trained as an artist at the University of Wisconsin–Madison, her poetry is intensely visual. Her poetry has appeared in anthologies, literary journals, and magazines. Her artwork has appeared in galleries in Wisconsin and New Mexico.

Johanna DeMay spent her childhood in Mexico City. As an adult she settled in New Mexico. Her poems have appeared in various journals, including *Constellations*, which last year nominated her poem *Cycling in Indian Country* for a Pushcart Prize. In 2018 her work was incuded in the "Contest Edition" of *Passager*.

Bruce Dethlefsen, Wisconsin Poet Laureate (2011-2012), has several poetry books published, plays in a couple of bands, volunteers in prison with writing workshops, and lives in Westfield, Wisconsin.

Marisa Frasca is the author of *Via Incanto, Poems from the Darkroom*, and forthcoming *Wild Fennel* (Bordighera Press). Her poems and translations have been widely published in literary journals and anthologies, among them: *Voices in Italian Americana*, *The Stillwater Review*, the *Journal of Italian Translation*. Born in Vittoria, Italy, Frasca resides in Manhasset, NY.

Kathryn Gahl's past lives include model, barkeep, registered nurse, single parent, teacher, and trauma survivor. Now a writer and storyteller, she dances ballroom and befriends many. Her multi-genre works have won awards from *Glimmer Train*, *Margie*, *Talking Writing*, *The Mill*, *New Millennium Writings*, The Hal Prize, *Chautauqua*, and *Wisconsin People & Ideas*.

Steven Golden is a retired police and fire dispatcher who has taken up poetry as a late-life avocation. He travels for spiritual exploration, when he is not otherwise residing in California and Arizona. He also returns at intervals to his alma mater, Lakeland University, in Sheboygan, WI.

Jeremy Griffin is the author of two story collections: *A Last Resort for Desperate People: Stories and a Novella*, from SFASU Press, and *Oceanography*, forthcoming from Orison Books. He teaches at Coastal Carolina University, where he serves as faculty fiction editor of *Waccamaw: a Journal of Contemporary Literature*.

Annette Langlois Grunseth, a descendant of hearty Norwegian women, continues the family legacy through words. Her chapbook, *Becoming Trans-Parent, One Family's Journey of Gender Transition* (Finishing Line Press) was nominated for a Pushcart Prize. Her poems have been recognized with *Wisconsin Academy Review*, *Wisconsin People & Ideas*, and the Wisconsin Fellowship of Poets. Learn more at annettegrunseth.com

Beth Gulley is a Kansas poet who loves to travel. While she spends most of her time teaching English at Johnson County Community College, she spent the 2016-2017 school year in Xi'an, China and her winter holiday 2018 in Pakistan. She has poetry in *The Thorny Locust* and *Aperion Review*.

John Guzlowski's *Echoes of Tattered Tongues*, a book about his parents' experiences as slave laborers in Nazi Germany, won the 2017 Franklin Award and the Eric Hoffer Award. He is the author of the *Hank and Marvin* mysteries and is a columnist for the *Dziennik Zwiazkowy*, America's oldest Polish newspaper.

Patrick Cabello Hansel has published poems and stories in over 50 journals, including *subprimal*, *Ilanot Review*, *Ash & Bones* and *Lunch Ticket*. His novella *Searching* was serialized in 33 issues of *The Alley News*. His poetry collection *The Devouring Land* is available from Main Street Rag Publishing.

Juleigh Howard-Hobson is an immigrant to the U.S. Her poetry has appeared in *Valparaiso Poetry Review*, *The Lyric*, *Able Muse*, *Weaving the Terrain* (Dos Gatos), and many other places. Nominations include Best of the Net, The Pushcart Prize, and The Rhysling Award. Her latest book is *Our Otherworld* (Red Salon).

Maryann Hurtt has always loved cooking, eating, & writing—she believes food and words bring us all closer together. In 2019, she will be traveling to Vietnam and hopes to write and eat like a wild woman. Check out her chapbook *River* and her website for more poems—maryannhurtt.com

Emalie Kamin is a 20-year-old student, currently studying English with the hopes of being a writer. She loves the outdoors and animals of all kinds.

Martha Jackson Kaplan is a Pushcart Prize nominated poet and flash fiction writer living in Madison, WI. She often meditates about history, color, a sense of place, and how those things reflect who we are. She can be found at marthakaplanpoet.com.

Poet and essayist **Rick Kempa** lives in Rock Springs, Wyoming. Recently retired after thirty years of teaching at Western Wyoming College, he has embarked on a path of full-time writing and walking. For more info, please see www.rickkempa.com

Winner of *North American Review*'s Hearst Prize and past President of the Wisconsin Fellowship of Poets, **Michael Kriesel** is the poetry editor of *Rosebud* magazine. Pebblebrook Press recently published his full-length collection *Zen Amen: abecedarians*. Read his electronic chapbook of short poems *Every Name in the Book* at http://www.righthandpointing.net/michael-kriesel-every-name

Dr. Jennifer Lagier has published fifteen books, edits the *Homestead Review*, and helps coordinate Monterey Bay Poetry Consortium readings. Newest books: *Harbingers* (Blue Light Press), *Camille Abroad*, *Like a B Movie*, *Camille Mobilizes* (FutureCycle Press). Forthcoming: *Trumped Up Election* (Xi Draconis Books). Visit her website: jlagier.net

Dr. Carrie La Seur is the award-winning author of two novels from William Morrow: *The Home Place* (2014) and *The Weight of an Infinite Sky* (2018). Her fiction, poetry, reviews, and essays appear in the *Guardian*; *Kenyon Review Online*; *Rumpus*; *Salon*, and more. She lives in Montana.

Olga Livshin is a Russian-American poet and translator. Her work has appeared in *The Kenyon Review, Poetry International*, and other journals. A full-length collection of poems and translations is forthcoming from Poets & Traitors Press. She is a writing coach and private poetry teacher and works with clients nationwide. Find her online at olgalivshin.com.

Bobbie Lee Lovell is the author of *Proposition at the Walk-In Infinity Chamber* (Finishing Line Press, 2017) and the mother of two teenagers, one of whom is an immigrant. Her professional skills include graphic design and print production.

Recently nominated for a Pushcart Prize in poetry, **Tracey Ludvik** has published numerous poems in many anthologies and journals. An educator and journalist, she has a B. A. degree in English from the University of Oregon and M.A. degree from Oregon State University.

Enesa Mahmić (1989, Bosnia and Herzegovina) is a travel writer based in Slovenia. She has published four poetry collections. Her poetry has appeared in many journals including *Azahar revista poetica, Words and Worlds, ŞİİR,* and *Dubai Poetics*. She is a member of the PEN Center.

Isabel Martinez is a 13-year-old seventh-grade student at Washington Junior High School in Manitowoc, WI. She is the oldest of five siblings, including one sister and three brothers. She wrote the poem that appears here after her father was deported to Mexico in 2012.

Jenny McBride's writing has appeared in *SLAB, Common Ground Review, Rappahannock Review, Streetwise, Conclave, The California Quarterly,* and other publications. She makes her home in the rainforest of southeast Alaska.

Jeri McCormick, who lives in Madison, Wisconsin, taught creative writing in senior centers and the Elderhostel program for twenty-five years. She co-authored *Writers Have No Age* (two editions by Haworth Press). She has been awarded writing fellowships, regional and international prizes, and her work has appeared in many magazines. Her most recent book is *Marrowbone of Memory*, published by Salmon Poetry in Ireland.

Aline Mello is a writer and editor living in Atlanta. She's from Brazil and spends much of her time volunteering with immigrant students. She is an Undocupoet fellow and her work has been published or is upcoming in *The New Republic, Atlanta Review, Grist* and elsewhere.

Amy Murre lives and works near the shores of Lake Michigan in southeastern Wisconsin. She writes poetry and prose, creates art, tends to family and animals, and teaches at Milwaukee School of Engineering. Her poetry has appeared in *Borderlands: Texas Poetry Review, Melusine, We'Moon,* and *Stoneboat Literary Journal,* among others. (For the curious, Murre is pronounced like Murry.)

Toti O'Brien is the Italian Accordionist with the Irish Last Name. She was born in Rome then moved to Los Angeles, where she makes a living as a self-employed artist, performing musician and professional dancer. Her work has recently appeared in *Colorado Boulevard, CultureCult, Metafore,* and *Gyroscope*.

Shelley Puhak is a poet and writer from Baltimore. She is the author of two books of poetry, the more recent of which is *Guinevere in Baltimore*. Her work has recently appeared in *The Atlantic*, *The Iowa Review*, and *Verse Daily*.

Georgia Ressmeyer, twice nominated for a Pushcart Prize in poetry, has published three books, the most recent of which is *Home/Body* (Pebblebrook Press). Her poetry has received awards from the Council for Wisconsin Writers, Wisconsin People & Ideas, the Wisconsin Fellowship of Poets, the Washington Island Literary Festival, Peninsula Pulse, and others.

Mary C. Rowin's poetry has appeared in *Panopoly*, *Stoneboat Literary Journal*, *Hummingbird*, and *Oakwood Literary Magazine*. Recent awards include poetry prizes from The Nebraska Writers Guild, and *Journal from the Heartland*. Mary's poem *Centering*, published in the Winter 2018 issue of *Blue Heron Review*, was nominated for the Pushcart Anthology. Mary lives with her husband in Middleton, Wisconsin.

Scott Allen Schmidt is a preacher's son, former rock n' roll front man, lyricist with more than three dozen songwriting credits to his name, poet, actor, father, and grandfather. His love affair with words was fostered from an early age through reading and listening to his father's sermons in a small church in the woods of Northern Wisconsin.

Paula Schulz has taught grade K3 through college and has been involved in several ekphrastic projects. She has poetry forthcoming in *The Anglican Review*. She lives and writes in Slinger, Wisconsin.

John Sierpinski has published poetry in many literary magazines such as *California Quarterly*, *North Coast Review*, and *Spectrum* to name a few. His work is also in six anthologies. He has been a Pushcart Prize nominee. His poetry collection, *Sucker Hole*, was published by Cholla Needles Press. He lives in California.

Jesse Simnegar is a 21-year-old Persian-American poet, songwriter, and producer from San Francisco, California. At sixteen, he was a finalist in Youth Speaks Teen Poetry Slam, and represented the Bay Area at *Brave New Voices* in Philadelphia. His writing explores mental health, displacement, family, ethnicity, and identity.

Sheryl Slocum lives in Milwaukee, Wisconsin, where she teaches English as a second language. Her poetry appears in numerous small press magazines and in the anthologies *No*, *Achilles*, and *Masquerades and Misdemeanors*. Sheryl is a member of the Hartford Avenue Poets and the Wisconsin Fellowship of Poets.

Pantea Amin Tofangchi is an Iranian-American poet, writer and graphic designer. She is the Art Director and graphic designer for *Passager* and Passager Books. She writes poems (in English), essays, stories and plays (mostly in Persian.) Her work has been published in *Welter*, *Little Patuxent Review*, *Ploughshares*, *Atlanta Review* in which she won the International Merit Award, and other journals. She was selected as a finalist for The National Poetry Series 2016.

Peggy Trojan lives in Brule, Wisconsin. She has published three chapbooks and a full collection. Her latest publication is *All That Matters, Collected Poems 2010-2018*. She is a member of the Wisconsin Fellowship of Poets.

Social issues are a major focus for Milwaukee poet **Phyllis Wax**. Her poems have been widely published online and in print. She has been nominated for the Pushcart Prize, as well as the Best of the Net and Bettering American Poetry anthologies.

Tad Phippen Wente, Port Washington, Wisconsin is learning, with age, how extensively poets' voices have fueled her writing journey ever since childhood. Her poems have appeared in several Wisconsin publications.

Ed Werstein, a regional VP of the Wisconsin Fellowship of Poets, was awarded the 2018 Lorine Niedecker Poetry Prize by the Council For Wisconsin Writers. His work has appeared in *Stoneboat Literary Journal*, *Blue Collar Review*, *Gyroscope Review*, and other publications. His book-length manuscript, *A Tar Pit To Dye In*, is available from Kelsay Books.

John Sibley Williams is the author of *As One Fire Consumes Another* (Orison Poetry Prize) and *Skin Memory* (Backwaters Prize). A nineteen-time Pushcart Prize nominee and winner of various awards, John serves as editor of *The Inflectionist Review*. Publications include: *Yale Review*, *Atlanta Review*, *Prairie Schooner*, *Massachusetts Review*, and *Third Coast*.

Rob Williams co-edited the Lambda Literary Award-Nominated anthology, *From Boys to Men: Gay Men Write About Growing Up*. He received his MFA in Fiction from Columbia University. His writing has appeared in *Versal*, *Maisonneuve*, *San Diego Citybeat* and more. He lives and teaches English and Creative Writing in San Francisco.

Marilyn Zelke Windau believes it is important to travel at any age, but especially when young. To meet and interact with people of other cultures—learn their history, see their monuments—expands one's own life. Travel has influenced her life and her writing. She is the author of four books of poetry, most recently *Hiccups Haunt Wilson Avenue* (Kelsay Books).

From 1990-91 and 1993-2001 **Mark Zimmermann** lived in Japan, working as a teacher and journalist. His poetry collection *Impersonations* was published by Pebblebrook Press in 2015. He lives with his wife Carole in Milwaukee, where he teaches at the Milwaukee School of Engineering. Currently he is working on a poetry manuscript based on his life in Japan.

About the Editors

Dawn Hogue is a Wisconsin writer who lives near Lake Michigan. Her poetry has appeared in *Inscape Magazine, Stoneboat Literary Journal, Making it Speak: Poets & Artists in Cahoots!, Intersections: Art & Poetry, Van Gogh Dreams,* and the *Wisconsin Fellowship of Poets 2018 Calendar*. She won the Hal Prize for poetry in 2017. Her debut novel, *A Hollow Bone*, is available from Water's Edge Press. Learn more at dawnhogue.com

Lisa Vihos is the poetry and arts editor of *Stoneboat Literary Journal*, an occasional guest blogger for *The Best American Poetry,* and the Sheboygan organizer for 100 Thousand Poets for Change. She has received awards from Wisconsin People and Ideas, the Wisconsin Fellowship of Poets, and has two Pushcart Prize nominations. Her fourth chapbook, *Fan Mail from Some Flounder*, was published in 2018 by Main Street Rag Publishing. Learn more at lisavihos.com

Coda

Persistence

In the dune sand atop a high shelf
of Lake Michgan's Sheboygan shoreline,
a scraggly juniper has crept about,
this way and that, looking for a foothold—
a thing I take for granted. Even my dog,
who has paused here to let the breeze
blow back her ears, who raises her muzzle to sniff,
finding a wisp of fish, the linger of last night,
pads her way over the golden ground without
taking a moment to consider every little stretch
the plant has made to sculpt itself even this far.
Not able to do more than set the shallowest
of roots, it nevertheless remains alive. When
now and then vicious winds have attacked
with scraping sand, it has persisted, webbing
its winding, barky roots upon inhospitable earth.

Citizens of the World

We are citizens of the world.
Our congress is the trees.
Their branches represent us
to the sky.

We are citizens of the earth.
We vote for the land.
It gives us our food,
a safe place to sleep.

We are citizens of the sea.
We are a new wave.
Upon us, rising—
the ship of our hearts.

www.ingramcontent.com/pod-product-compliance
Lightning Source LLC
Chambersburg PA
CBHW050441010526
44118CB00013B/1631